IMAGES
of America

SHILOH NATIONAL MILITARY PARK

On the Cover: Illinois had more troops at Shiloh than any other state. Once the Shiloh National Military Park was established in 1894, Illinois sent a commission to place monuments to its troops at the battlefield. The commission posed while at Shiloh in front of the large stacks of cannonballs and cannons awaiting placement on the field. (Courtesy of Shiloh National Military Park.)

IMAGES
of America

SHILOH NATIONAL MILITARY PARK

Brian K. McCutchen and Timothy B. Smith
foreword by Woody Harrell

ARCADIA
PUBLISHING

ISBN 978-0-7385-9135-3

Published by Arcadia Publishing
Charleston, South Carolina

Printed in the United States of America

Library of Congress Control Number: 2011938365

For all general information, please contact Arcadia Publishing:
Telephone 843-853-2070
Fax 843-853-0044
E-mail sales@arcadiapublishing.com
For customer service and orders:
Toll-Free 1-888-313-2665

Visit us on the Internet at www.arcadiapublishing.com

To all past and present Shiloh National Military Park employees, who have preserved the memory and the battlefield of Shiloh for future generations.

Contents

Foreword

A century and a half after the event it commemorates and 118 years after its designation as a national military park, Shiloh retains its reputation as America's best-preserved battlefield. Much of the credit for this status goes to Shiloh's battle veterans, who successfully lobbied Congress for the park's establishment. With support from both the North and South, they pursued the new idea of the nation acquiring and preserving the entire battlefield.

Like Chickamauga and Gettysburg, two other Civil War battlefields specifically mentioned in the law creating it, Shiloh National Military Park became part of a comprehensive system of battlefield parks. All were designed by Congress to preserve these major battlefields for historical and professional study but also to serve as lasting memorials to the great armies on either side of the Civil War. Just as the field of Gettysburg memorialized the Army of the Potomac and the Army of Northern Virginia, Shiloh was set aside so its veterans, the men of the US Armies of the Tennessee and Ohio and the Confederate Army of the Mississippi, might "have the history of one of their memorable battles preserved on the ground where they fought."

Shiloh's enabling legislation, signed by Pres. Grover Cleveland on December 27, 1894, delineates a boundary encompassing over 6,000 acres, authorizing the War Department to utilize "so much thereof as the commissioners of the park [Shiloh veterans themselves] may deem necessary . . . to ascertain and mark with historical tablets or otherwise . . . lines of battle of all troops engaged and the history of their movements in the battle." Following the watercourses surrounding the northern end of the plateau known as Shiloh Hill, the park's authorized boundary demonstrates the foresight of its founders by providing a natural buffer of the Tennessee River floodplain around Shiloh's most hallowed ground. This concept of a geographic boundary makes Shiloh unique among the major Civil War battlefields.

Shiloh had already existed as a national military park for two decades when the National Park Service was created in 1916, in an era when more park visitors still arrived by water than by land. The development of the Civil War parks under the War Department administration was approaching maturity 17 years later when all, including Shiloh, were transferred to the National Park Service. However, even with the proliferation of automobile travel in the last half of the 20th century, Shiloh's visitation lagged behind other important battle sites. In fact, not until the dawn of the 21st century did the local county's population finally surpass Shiloh's 23,746 battle casualties.

Over the years, this isolation has proved a double-edged sword in regard to Shiloh's preservation. The area's rural character has provided protection against the type of development threat long familiar to many Civil War battlefields in the east. Yet, over the years, its location and sparse population has produced few stakeholders to champion the needs of the park. The Civil War sesquicentennial offers a critical time to rally support to complete the preserved park envisioned by the Shiloh veterans.

Surviving photographic images of the Shiloh field contemporary with the April 1862 battle may be counted on one hand, with several fingers left over. The availability of photography changed dramatically over the next few months with the arrival of photographic studios, such as Armstead and White and Howard and Hill during the Union occupation of the nearby railroad junction at Corinth, Mississippi. Thankfully for Civil War historians, these photographers took time away from their portraiture to capture images of local landmarks, earthworks, camps, and battlefields. From then until today, the camera has recorded the park's continuing story, but these photographs have never been gathered in a central location. Compiling this historic album from both public and private sources provides a valuable resource to anyone interested in the commemoration of the first major battle in the Civil War's western theater. Hopefully it will help spur renewed interest in Shiloh's continued preservation.

—Woody Harrell
Superintendent
Shiloh National Military Park

ACKNOWLEDGMENTS

We wish to first and foremost acknowledge the help and encouragement of our wives, Sharon McCutchen and Kelly Smith, and for their support and patience as we pursued our respective careers in the field of history and preservation, and also for their "cheerleading" for completion of this book. Our children, Noah McCutchen, age 7, and Mary Kate and Leah Grace Smith, ages 4 and 2, also spent a great deal of time helping by bringing their respective daddies treats, encouragement, and hugs.

We also wish to thank friend and former colleague supervisory park ranger Ashley Berry of the Corinth Unit of Shiloh National Military Park for her invaluable assistance in accessing requested material and scanning historic photographs. Also, thanks to Supt. Woody Harrell, who has encouraged such a publication for many years and who provided the forward for this book. Our appreciation also goes to Stacy Allen, chief ranger and park historian, for granting research access to the vast Shiloh holdings and for his years of friendship and support. Unless otherwise indicated, all photographs in this book are courtesy of the Shiloh National Military Park.

We also thank those individuals who provided access to and use of their personal collections, including Dixie Donnell Decker, Jeff Wilkes, and John Ross, all of Savannah, Tennessee. Special appreciation also goes to Ronnie Brewington and Henry Williams of the Hardin County Historical Society for access to its vast collection of Shiloh-area photographs. Dr. Stacy Reaves, who provided historical details that we were missing as she completed research for a book on the monuments of Shiloh, actually began the process that resulted in this book. Lastly, special appreciation goes to Pamela Rempe and retired national park superintendent Gary Candelaria for their willingness to read the text and provide numerous suggestions. The detail of each was impeccable.

INTRODUCTION

"When a people renders such honors to the heroic dead it honors itself. The national care bestowed on this historic spot is as much a potent lesson to the future as a sacred duty to the past, for it commemorates the virtues without which nations cannot survive. May those who fell here never be forgotten, and may these monuments erected to their memory remain as enduring admonitions to the youth of succeeding generations, to love and serve their country equally as well."

—Basil Duke
Confederate veteran and Shiloh Commission member
May 17, 1904

Located on the west bank of the Tennessee River, only 20 miles or so from the Mississippi state line, the battlefield of Shiloh is a staple of familiarity to history buffs and Civil War devotees around the world. It is a landscape set aside for commemoration, preservation, and education, and since its establishment as a national military park in 1894, it has been a place where visitors can learn about and walk the ground of one of America's bloodiest battles.

The April 6 and 7, 1862, engagement near Pittsburg Landing, better known as Shiloh, was arguably America's first modern battle. Consisting of almost 110,000 participants and nearly 24,000 casualties, the isolated battle that was fought in rural southwest Tennessee shocked the nation and indicated the tragic direction American warfare was heading. Unfortunately, the conflict continued on, lasting another three years.

Even as the war progressed, life for Shiloh's local inhabitants returned to the struggling subsistence farming of the area's poor clay and gravel soil. Trees shattered and clipped by the intensity of small arms and artillery fire dotted the landscape. Tons of iron and lead littered the ground in all directions, and, most hauntingly, thousands of human remains were buried across the areas of heaviest combat.

Fortunately, the first phase of Shiloh's commemoration occurred only some four years after the battle—the creation of the Pittsburg Landing National Cemetery. As part of the newly created national cemetery system, the burial ground provided a place of honorable internment for primarily Union battle dead who were originally buried on the field on which they died. Located atop the bluff at Pittsburg Landing, the cemetery soon witnessed an increase in visitation, often with family members seeking the burial place of a loved one. As the years passed, visitation by aging battle survivors also increased. Many veterans wished to share of their battlefield exploits or attend reunions; others came to find emotional closure.

During one reunion visit in 1893, appalled veterans who learned that it was still not uncommon to unearth remains of battle dead took the first steps to preserve the entire field of Shiloh. The timing of the conversation coincided with activities at battlefields to the east, where the US government was acquiring fields such as Antietam, Chickamauga-Chattanooga, and Gettysburg for the purpose of preservation and commemoration. For Shiloh, that initial discussion on a steamboat in the Tennessee River produced a major preservation effort, and on December 27, 1894, Shiloh National Military Park became a reality.

Although administratively under the jurisdiction of the US War Department, the park's first set of overseers was a three-man commission made up of veterans of the battle. In many respects, the newly established battlefield park was thus a monument by veterans to veterans. With minimal appropriations but great political clout, the commission soon began making surveys and acquiring land. Perhaps as important, the commission secretary and historian Maj. David Wilson Reed began to research and interview veterans. Ultimately, he institutionalized what became the official Shiloh story for more than half a century. Reed's influence was unprecedented in the initial development and presentation of the battle's story, and his clout remains fully visible today.

Soon, the battlefield as we know it today began to take shape. As designated in the enabling legislation, all states that had units in the battle were authorized to place monuments or memorials on the landscape. From 1899 through the first decades of the 20th century, monuments large and small, most made of stone and bronze, began to dot the countryside. The memorial statues, many of them allegorical figures, were more than artistic sculpture, however; they were the representative embodiment of the very soldiers who wished to have their story conveyed in perpetuity. And with each monument dedication, the public orations of respected political figures illustrated a key commonality—reunification and camaraderie.

But the park's history was not without trouble. Almost 15 years into its development, a tragic tornado devastated much of the infrastructure, crashing monuments to the ground, destroying much of the national cemetery, and spreading the irreplaceable park library, maps, and correspondence over a 50-mile swath. Fortunately, out of the devastation rose a new, improved operation capable of meeting the growing needs of visitation.

There were other major changes brewing at Shiloh as well. The passing of the last members of the original park commission led to a new generation of management. Fortunately, DeLong Rice, the son of a Civil War veteran, entered his superintendent position fully respecting the hard work and mission of his predecessors. With such awareness, Rice sought to build upon the veterans' devotion while improving the park in many ways and making the story more understandable to those nonveteran generations that followed.

These changes occurring at Shiloh foreshadowed a larger context of transformation that soon engulfed the entire nation. By the mid-1930s, the full force of the Great Depression had burst onto the scene. Over the course of the next few years, many New Deal workers, including those of the Civilian Conservation Corps who constructed a camp and barracks on the western side of the park, made improvements to Shiloh's roads, bridges, landscape, and national cemetery. In the midst of such development, another major transition occurred—the military park and national cemetery went from the War Department to the 17-year-old National Park Service.

When the chaotic years of depression and war finally ended, efforts began again to update the interpretation of the Shiloh story. Most notably, Shiloh debuted a motion picture that, although made on a shoestring budget, served as the primary introduction to the battle for more than 55 years. Not surprisingly, the events commemorating the centennial of the war in the 1960s saw a resurgence in memorial activities, including the dedication of new monuments from Texas, Kentucky, Missouri, and eventually Tennessee.

Today, an expanded Shiloh National Military Park remains one of America's most revered and best-preserved battlefields. A popular slogan for the park pays homage to the undisturbed battle setting, stating: "Where you can still hear the cannon roar." For many visitors, this is quite accurate. Shiloh remains a place for true contemplation.

But it was the veterans of Shiloh who first established the military park to ensure their actions would not be forgotten, who built upon the landscape a true monument to themselves. It is now the responsibility of today's generation, and of those that follow, to carry forward the sacrifice and memory of 1862 far into the future and to ensure that the 4,000-plus acres of sacred ground truly remain an eternal place for commemoration, preservation, and education.

One

Shiloh

Bloody Battle in Tennessee

The Battle of Shiloh was one of the most horrific engagements of the Civil War, producing 23,746 official casualties, although the total number was almost certainly higher. Even above the carnage, the battle had other important ramifications as well. Coming as it did early in the conflict, Shiloh served to warn both North and South that the war was going to be long, grueling, and bloody. It also caused the nation to take a collective gasp, as casualties of that proportion had never before been seen in America. No less important, strategically, the battle opened the way for the eventual capture of Corinth, Mississippi, to the south, which was the reason for the battle in the first place. Intent on capturing the Confederate railroads that converged there, the Union armies fought the major battle for those railroads at Shiloh.

The fighting was no less significant for the battlefield itself and the people who lived on it. Most lost homes, some lost lives, and all were affected in one way or another. The results did not end with the conclusion of the battle, either. The locals, most of whom had left by the time the fighting began, returned to desolation. Even worse, their farms were now vast cemeteries, as the dead had been buried on the field itself.

The result would be a permanent change at Shiloh, first as the battle left its horrid toll and then as the federal government erected a permanent national cemetery at Shiloh. The fame of the place would also add to that change, as thousands of veterans would return to the battlefield to see their scene of conflict over the decades, eventually with formal veteran reunions taking place. Few such isolated areas saw similar visitation, but because Shiloh played such a critical role in the nation's history, it would never be the same.

The Battle of Shiloh took its name from the small Methodist church located on the battlefield. There are no contemporary photographs of the actual church, but this postwar painting indicates how it likely looked. Although heavily damaged, the church itself survived the battle but not the war. Sources differ on its demise, but the Union army probably took its logs and boards for firewood and bridge-building material.

The Cherry Mansion in Savannah, Tennessee, was the headquarters of Union commanding general Ulysses S. Grant. It was here that Grant first heard the sounds of battle on the morning of April 6, 1862. The Shiloh National Military Park had an opportunity to buy the house at one time, but it is still privately owned. (Courtesy of Jeff Wilkes.)

Maj. Gen. Ulysses S. Grant commanded the Union Army of the Tennessee at Shiloh. He recovered from the Confederate surprise attack to win a major victory and went on to become the North's best general. He captured Vicksburg, relieved Chattanooga, and fought Robert E. Lee to a standstill, accepting his surrender at Appomattox. He later became the 18th president of the United States.

Maj. Gen. Don Carlos Buell commanded the Union Army of the Ohio at Shiloh. Marching from Nashville to join Grant's army for an attack on Corinth, Mississippi, Buell's lead divisions arrived at Shiloh late on the first day of the battle. Buell's men then counterattacked with Grant's the next day. In the 1890s, Buell was one of the government-appointed commissioners overseeing the Shiloh National Military Park. (Courtesy of Library of Congress.)

Although arguably neither the most vicious nor the most important tactical action at the battle of Shiloh, the most famous fighting on the battlefield raged in the Hornet's Nest and Sunken Road, which Confederates so named because the bullets flying past their ears sounded like angry hornets. Emphasis on that area of the fighting grew in the postwar years as veterans of the Hornet's Nest, including Union general Benjamin Prentiss, touted their accomplishments in speeches, books, and media creations. Most significantly, a large panorama painting of the battle that appeared in the mid-1880s depicted the fighting at Shiloh, focusing on the Hornet's Nest. This is one of the scenes from that painting. Later, the national park's first historian, David W. Reed, institutionalized the Hornet's Nest as an icon. Over the years, the story of fighting in the Hornet's Nest grew, and today, it is regarded in popular opinion as the key to the battle. (Courtesy of *Battles and Leaders*.)

Confederate general Albert Sidney Johnston commanded the Army of the Mississippi at Shiloh. He was well regarded as the South's best general early in the war, although his prestige had declined some because of the defeats in Tennessee prior to Shiloh. He launched the surprise attack as a great gamble and died during the fighting. Johnston is the highest-ranking American military officer ever to die in combat. (Courtesy of Library of Congress.)

Confederate general P.G.T. Beauregard, Johnston's second in command at Shiloh, took over the army when Johnston bled to death on the battlefield. He became engrossed in controversy when he called off the Confederate attacks that evening, thinking he had the victory won and could easily finish the triumph the next morning. But Union reinforcements arrived during the night, causing many to conclude that Beauregard had thrown away a victory. (Courtesy of Library of Congress.)

The US Navy played a critical role at Shiloh. Gunboats patrolled the river and also engaged the enemy during the first day's action, most notably at the end of the fighting and during the night. The USS *Tyler* and USS *Lexington* are seen here in action. While tactically important, their best service was in giving the North a psychological advantage. Many Confederates spoke in fear of the gunboats. (Courtesy of *Battles and Leaders*.)

After the battle, there was massive evidence that a momentous event had taken place at Shiloh. Burials, debris, and lead-filled trees marked the site of the battle. In one novel occurrence, a soldier carved his initials into a tree, and the evidence, as seen here, was still legible many decades afterwards.

One of only three contemporary photographs from the battlefield of Shiloh, this view of Pittsburg Landing shows Union steamboats tied up on the river immediately after the battle. Many vessels brought in supplies and troops, while others took away wounded soldiers. A small cabin at the landing can be seen at left. (Courtesy of *Dedication of Monuments to Iowa Soldiers.*)

A slightly different angle of the same scene above, this view shows Grant's headquarters boat, *Tigress*, in the center. It was on this boat that Grant rushed to Pittsburg Landing on the morning of April 6, 1862. The *Tigress* later sank at Vicksburg. One of the wooden gunboats can also be seen in the background.

Probably the most iconic contemporary illustration of Shiloh, this is one of only three known photographs of the Shiloh battlefield, although there were likely more taken at the time. This view is especially valuable because of the guns, the attending soldiers, and the precise location of the view. Obviously taken after the battle ended, the photograph shows the siege guns of an Illinois battery, brought to Pittsburg Landing for use against Corinth, Mississippi. When the Confederates surprised the Union army at Shiloh, Grant ordered every gun to be put into his final line to defend the landing, the major source of reinforcements. These guns were in action during the final stage of the first day's fighting and then proceeded with the army to Corinth later in May. There is some speculation, given the placing of the earthworks, the campsites in the rear, and the general lay of the land, that this image may be reversed. (Courtesy of *Illinois at Shiloh*.)

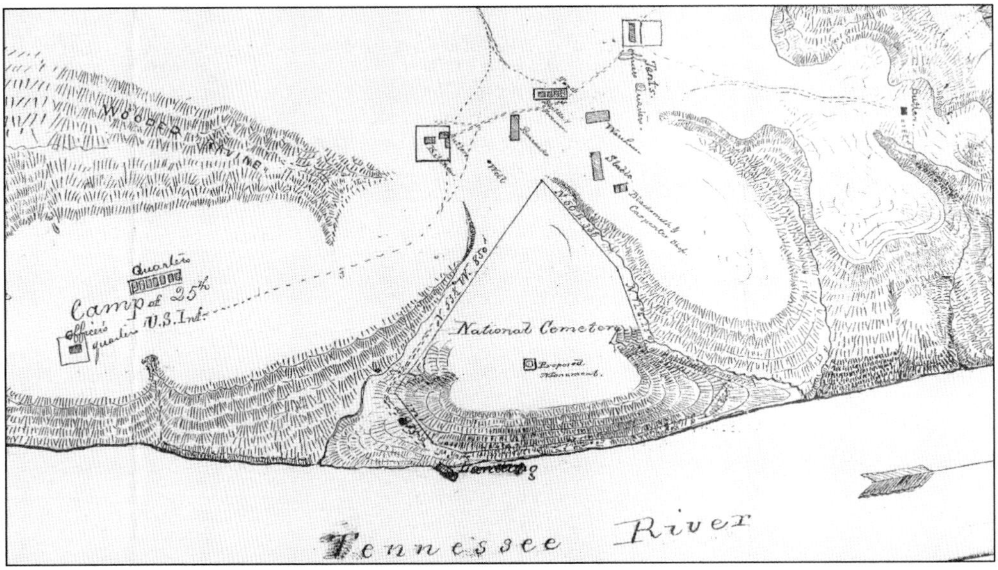

The battlefield of Shiloh became calm again once the armies moved southward. After the conflict ended, the federal government began building national cemeteries to hold the Union dead. One of these was at Shiloh. This map shows the position of the cemetery on the bluffs overlooking the river as well as the camps of the 25th US Infantry. (Courtesy of National Archives.)

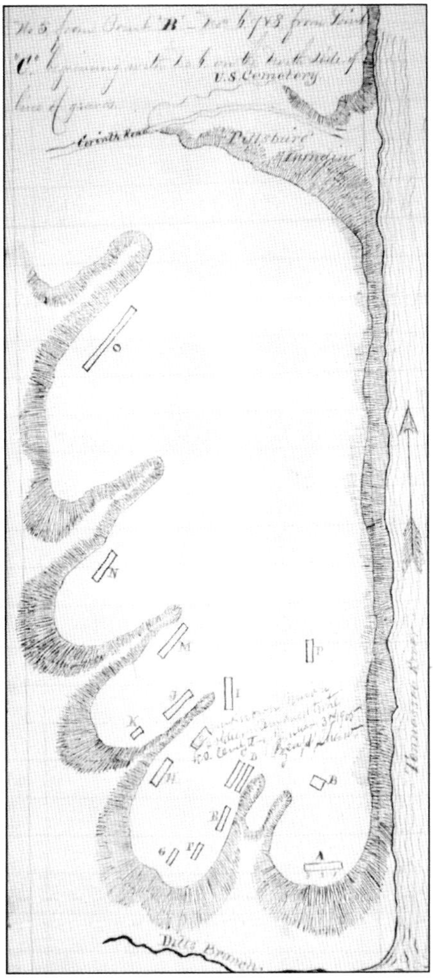

In 1866, burial details scoured the battlefield of Shiloh looking for Union soldiers buried hurriedly in the days after the battle. Unlike the vast majority of the Confederate dead, they were to be dug up and reburied in the beautiful national cemetery at the landing. The crews often drew maps of the original burial locations. This view shows some of the original burial places near Pittsburg Landing.

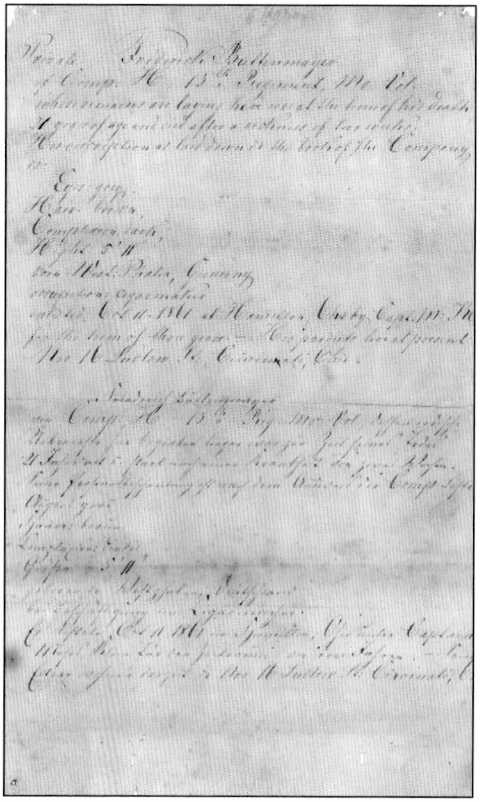
Private Frederick Buttenmayer
of Comp. H 13th Regiment, Mo. Vol.

Most of the Union soldiers reinterred in Shiloh National Cemetery are unknown. For those who are known, the burial crews used various methods of identification, but one of the best was when there was an identifying document on the body. This document, in both English and German, was found on the body of Pvt. Frederick Buttenmayer of Company H, 13th Missouri Infantry.

Because of the care taken to record Buttenmayer's identity at the time of his burial in 1862, he is one of the small percentage of soldiers identified in the Shiloh National Cemetery. Today, his headstone, seen at right, is in Section G of the cemetery, overlooking the Tennessee River. Originally marked with wooden headboards, Buttenmayer and the others interred in the national cemetery received permanent marble headstones in the 1870s. (Courtesy of Brian K. McCutchen.)

Probably the most novel way a deceased soldier's burial place was identified is the example of J.D. Putnam. Burial crews in 1866 were able to identify Putnam because his comrades had carved his name in the base of a tree where he was buried. Years later, the State of Wisconsin placed a monument in the exact spot, seen at right, patterned after the surviving stump.

J.D. Putnam was hit and killed in the second day's fighting, but the careful work his comrades took in identifying his burial place assured he would be one of the known burials in the cemetery. Today, Putnam rests under a large oak tree in the Shiloh National Cemetery, in the burial plot reserved for members of the 14th Wisconsin Infantry. (Courtesy of Brian K. McCutchen.)

Once the work of reburying the Union dead in the national cemetery began, the War Department also began to build infrastructural facilities at the cemetery. The crews built a cemetery lodge as well as other outbuildings. This drawing of the office and shed is the earliest known rendering of the Shiloh National Cemetery. (Courtesy of National Archives.)

As the soldiers were reinterred in the cemetery, the example of Henry Burke is illustrative of the effort to cause visitors to think about what the cemetery represented. Although probably a musician in his 20s named Heinrich Budke, the soldier was given the name Burke, labeled as a drummer, and placed at the entrance to the cemetery. The idea of the sacrifice of a little American drummer boy still tugs at visitors even today. (Courtesy of Jeff Wilkes.)

In the years after the battle, the local citizens of the Shiloh battlefield, most of whom had fled their homes prior to the fighting, returned to their land and rebuilt their lives. Most, but not all, of the cabins and outbuildings had been damaged or destroyed during the fighting, and their property was now a wasteland riddled with the debris of battle as well as thousands of human remains. Yet they made the best of their situation. Here is an 1884 view of one of the surviving structures on the battlefield, the Sarah Bell cabin. Located on the Hamburg-Savannah Road, this cabin sat just south of the famous Peach Orchard. It was near here that Albert Sidney Johnston received his mortal wound, and he died in a ravine just across the road. Unfortunately, the people in this scene are unidentified.

Other structures survived the fighting as well, particularly those on the edges of the field of battle. This view shows a dogtrot house. By the time the Shiloh National Military Park was established in 1894, there were only a few surviving structures, and they were not in the best of condition, as evidenced in this view.

Residents of the Shiloh battlefield interpreted the engagement prior to the establishment of the national park. Unfortunately, they sometimes relied on legend, as in the case of Albert Sidney Johnston's death site. Citizens stated Johnston died near the tree shown in this photograph. The later park historian verified the actual location as across the road and to the south, although there is still some debate over the issue. (Courtesy of Jeff Wilkes.)

By the 1890s, veterans of both the Blue and the Gray were beginning to pass away at an increasing rate, and a distinct feeling of nostalgia and reconciliation began to emerge, prompting them to return to their battle sites and later to preserve them for posterity. The veterans sought to heal old wounds caused by years of arguing over slavery and states' rights as well as from the war and reconstruction. Many did so through veteran reunions. The battlefields were prime locations for these reunions, and Shiloh saw its share. Veterans of both sides flocked to the battlefield, and it was on one of these excursions in 1893 that the idea of creating a national military park at Shiloh emerged. Pictured here is a group of veterans at Shiloh Spring in 1895. The top of Shiloh Church can barely be seen in the background.

By the time the Shiloh National Military Park was established in 1894, the battlefield was in dire need of preservation. Locals still lived on the field, and a few lived in historic battle-era cabins. But many of the old artifacts and witnesses to the battle were destroyed or damaged by then. One example was the William Manse George cabin. Originally sitting on the western side of the battlefield, the cabin was moved to the Peach Orchard area just weeks after the battle by George, whose own cabin had been destroyed during the fighting. His family and others inhabited the cabin for decades, but by the turn of the century, it was terrible shape, despite being a historic structure that witnessed the battle. The dilapidated condition of the cabin around the time of the park's establishment is evident.

Two

NATIONAL MILITARY PARK

SHILOH'S GOLDEN AGE

America's preservation mentality took a drastic turn in 1890, having a direct impact on the Shiloh battlefield. In that year, the federal government first became heavily involved in battlefield preservation, with Congress establishing the Chickamauga and Chattanooga National Military Park. That action set the stage and provided a template for other parks in the future. Five battlefields were eventually preserved to varying degrees in the 1890s, Chickamauga and Chattanooga, Antietam, Shiloh, Gettysburg, and Vicksburg, with many others to come in the decades thereafter. The process is still occurring today.

Shiloh National Military Park was established in 1894. The US secretary of war was tasked with oversight of the park, like the others, but the enabling legislation mandated a three-man commission of veterans would actually oversee the battlefield park. This commission, appointed in 1895, was the first manager of the Shiloh park and as such made many key decisions about how the park would develop, what it would look like, what events and places would be emphasized, and whose version of the story would be followed when conflict arose. It was an extremely important job that controlled many ramifications, such as the reconciliation of the veterans that would take place on the battlefield, the preservation of hallowed ground, and the actual development of a collective national memory concerning the battle.

The commission's membership changed over time as veterans passed away or resigned, but the three major decision makers were chairman of the commission Cornelius Cadle of Iowa, commission historian David W. Reed, also of Iowa, and park engineer Atwell Thompson, a younger immigrant from Ireland. These three men put their stamp on how Shiloh developed in the early commission era as the park went from an isolated and barren wilderness to a memorial to which tens of thousands of people flocked each year. The resulting development of infrastructure and commemorative features, such as roads, bridges, monuments, and tablets, was a testament to the hard work of these commissioners as well as the federal government's belief in the importance of the battlefield of Shiloh.

The focal point of the newly established park was Pittsburg Landing, just as it had been for the contending armies decades earlier. Most visitors came and went through the landing, as did most of the goods for the park and the surrounding countryside. This view shows cotton bales waiting to be shipped. (Courtesy of *Illinois at Shiloh*.)

Over time, the main commodity unloaded at Pittsburg Landing by boat changed from goods to people. Prior to the battle and especially the park, few had reason to stop at the landing. Once the park came into being, tens of thousands of visitors flocked to the site each year. This novel view shows a steamboat docked at the landing. (Courtesy of Jeff Wilkes.)

One of the most famous packet boats on the Tennessee River, the stern-wheel paddleboat *Clyde* frequented Pittsburg Landing, bringing visitors as well as memorial items bounds for the park. Most of the monumentation, cannons, tablets, and equipment at Shiloh came by riverboat and was unloaded at the landing. (Courtesy of *The Seventy-Seventh Pennsylvania at Shiloh.*)

Pittsburg Landing was a special place of remembrance for veterans who returned to the battlefield. The vast majority of the Union soldiers at Shiloh had come onto the battlefield at the landing. The Confederates were likewise cognizant of its importance. Decades later, the landing was a place of reconciliation, as seen in this view of veterans embracing each other warmly. (Courtesy of Jeff Wilkes.)

One of the first places visitors encountered after arriving at the landing was the Shiloh National Cemetery. In the center of the circular layout was a rostrum, from which speeches were given. It also made a wonderful backdrop for family and friends' photographs, as seen in this view in 1897.

One of the most iconic photographs of Shiloh National Cemetery, this view shows visitors at the entrance of the grounds. The rows and rows of headstones denote the symmetrical layout of the cemetery. The grave of a supposed drummer boy, seen in the foreground, alerted all who entered that this was hallowed ground.

This view of Shiloh National Cemetery shows the western portion of the grounds with its even rows, ornamental decorations, and monumentation. Also evident in the foreground is the massive stone wall that encircled the cemetery, as well as the administration buildings to the left. Interestingly, two of the stones in this section were for Confederates, although no reason for their inclusion was ever given.

This view of the cemetery shows the graves on the very bluff of the river, situated as to let all who passed know this was a solemn location. The US flag that fluttered from the mast similarly let all know that the nation was reunited. Note the large naval mortar near the mast, which would later be placed overlooking the river, where its remains today.

This view of the cemetery looking toward the river illustrates the layout. The inner circle is surrounded by larger sections of graves, with individual regimental burial sites around the periphery. The regimental burial plots, facilitated by the burial of many of the soldiers originally by regiment, are unique items of the Shiloh cemetery. Note the tablets with the poem "Bivouac of the Dead," which was standard at all national cemeteries.

Situated in the cemetery itself was one of the most historic sites on the battlefield. Ulysses S. Grant made his headquarters under this large tree during the battle, which he explained in detail in his memoirs. The trunk of the tree was still standing when the park came into being, although it was soon toppled by a storm. A monument now marks the spot.

To oversee the Shiloh National Cemetery, the War Department had a superintendent on site. He lived and worked in the administration building, actually within the cemetery itself. This lodge, the second at the cemetery, greeted visitors during the initial construction of the park in the 1890s. It was later replaced by another, which still stands today.

Many commemorative events took place in the national cemetery, especially on Memorial Day in May of each year. Illustrating the reconciliation in which the national park and others like it played such a role, the park's Confederate commissioner, Robert F. Looney, is seen here addressing a crowd at the rostrum on Memorial Day in 1899.

Over time, Shiloh National Military Park became a favorite place for veteran reunions. This photograph shows Civil War veterans gathered at Shiloh Spring, just south of Shiloh Church. These veteran reunions played a major role in the creation of the park, with huge reunions taking place in 1894 and 1895. In addition, they played into the reconciliation of the era, with both sides coming together to jointly remember their war. The fact that the park itself memorialized the Confederate as well as Union soldiers, units, and dead said much about the reunification even then taking place, and that one of the three commissioners governing the park was a Confederate veteran convinced even more that the feelings of mutual admiration were real. The speeches that were given at these reunions and monument dedications fairly oozed with brotherly affection. Obviously, there was also a tangible result to the veterans returning to the battlefield; they spread out to find the old places where they had fought, thus documenting for later generations valuable historic localities.

This view of a veteran reunion illustrates the various people involved, such as women and children. This group is gathered around Shiloh Spring, one of many on the park that no doubt flowed with blood during the battle. Note the carriages and other conveyances at the top of the ridge.

In a day prior to automobiles, the chief way to tour the park was by horse-drawn carriage. Seen here is a large gathering of conveyances during a reunion, from simple farm wagons to nicer buggies. Visitors arriving by riverboat could often hire transportation for touring the park.

Many of the reunions, particularly Confederate ones, took place at Shiloh Church. Here is a group at the church in the 1890s. The original log building had not survived the war, but the congregation built another church in the late 1880s. Eventually, the members would build a modern church, which is still in use today.

The central entity governing the creation of the park, the monumentation, and the maintenance was the three-man commission of veterans who lived away from the park itself. Iowan Cornelius Cadle, center, was the commission chairman. Commissioner James H. Ashcraft of Kentucky is at right, with commission historian David W. Reed at left. Their wives often accompanied the veterans to the battlefield.

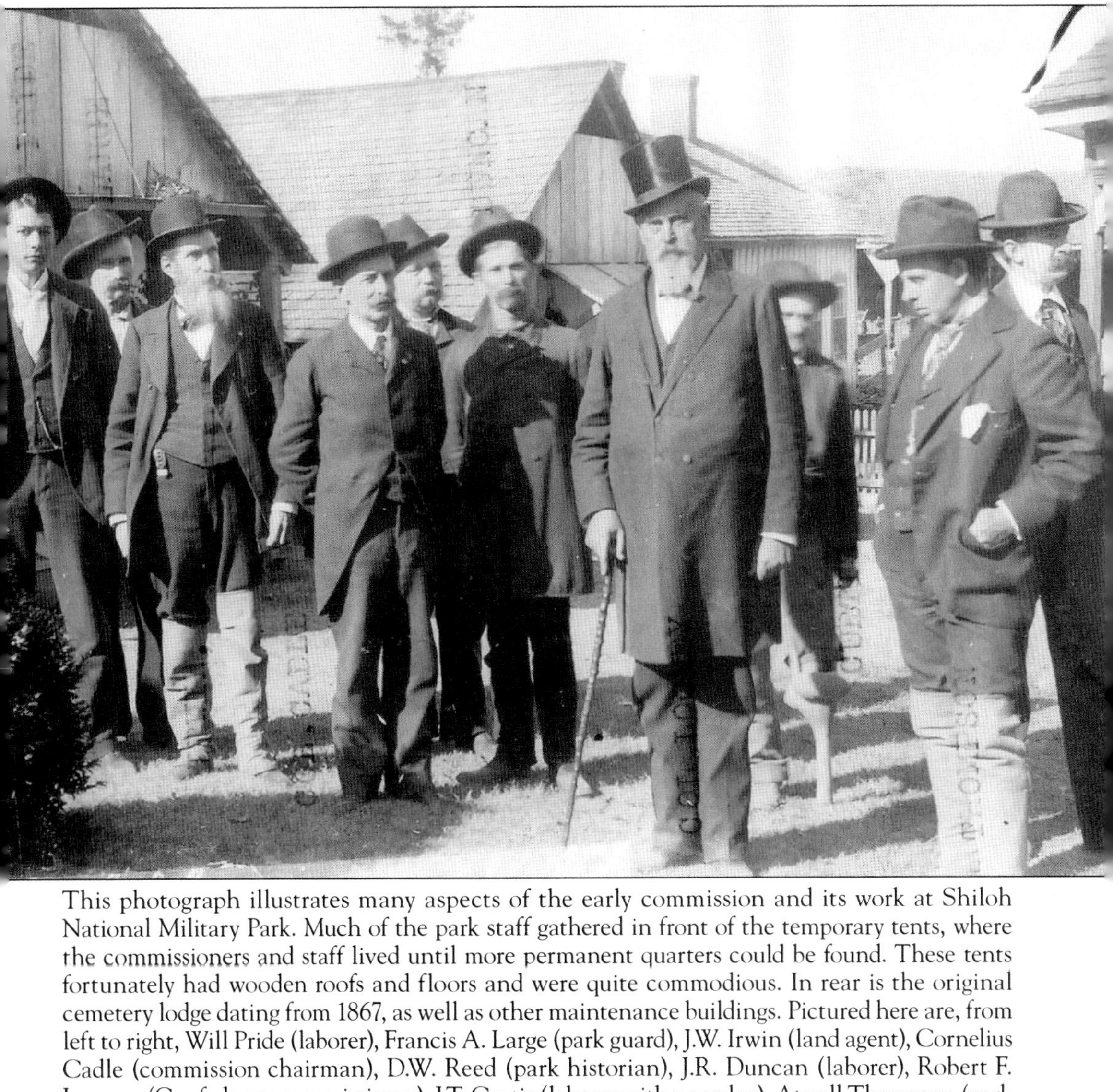

This photograph illustrates many aspects of the early commission and its work at Shiloh National Military Park. Much of the park staff gathered in front of the temporary tents, where the commissioners and staff lived until more permanent quarters could be found. These tents fortunately had wooden roofs and floors and were quite commodious. In rear is the original cemetery lodge dating from 1867, as well as other maintenance buildings. Pictured here are, from left to right, Will Pride (laborer), Francis A. Large (park guard), J.W. Irwin (land agent), Cornelius Cadle (commission chairman), D.W. Reed (park historian), J.R. Duncan (laborer), Robert F. Looney, (Confederate commissioner), J.T. Curtis (laborer with a peg leg), Atwell Thompson (park engineer), and M.A. Kirby (laborer).

The Shiloh commission's tents were situated near the cemetery lodge, in which the commission at first kept an office. The commissioners lived at their homes but traveled to Shiloh for various occasions such as reunions, to meet visiting dignitaries, and to periodically oversee the work. These tents became home, with the occupants' own touches. Reed, for example, placed a flag and nurtured a rose bush on his.

M.A. Kirby was an engineering laborer at Shiloh National Military Park, working on the surveying crew as a transit man with engineer Atwell Thompson. This view of his tent shows in detail the living conditions of the commission. Note the floored tent and the accessories inside, including a lamp and bed.

A festival atmosphere developed when the commission or other luminaries visited Shiloh. Pictured are three veterans of the battle, including Robert F. Looney, the Confederate commissioner, in the foreground. On the porch of the cemetery lodge is John A. McClernand (right), who had commanded a Union division in the battle, and someone identified only as Colonel Galbraith.

By far, the man who had the most impact on the way Shiloh National Military Park and the history of the battle developed was David W. Reed. As park historian, Reed wrote much of the text for the tablets and oversaw the monumentation of the park. He almost single-handedly instituted the Hornet's Nest theory at the park. He is seen here with his wife, Ellen.

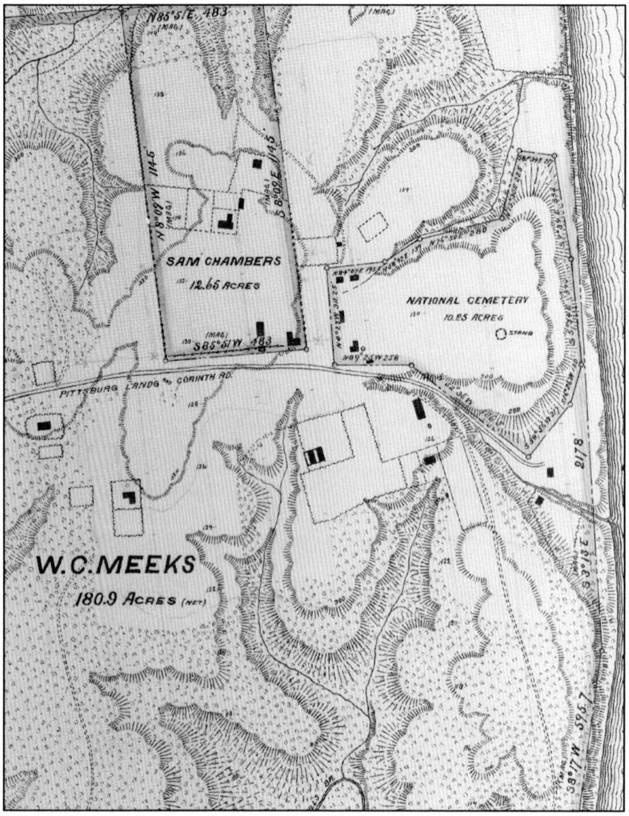

One of the first items of major business was to acquire the land on which the battle was fought. To make sense of the confusing land ownership, Atwell Thompson drew plot maps for each owner. This map shows the Pittsburg Landing area. Eventually, the park commission bought some 3,600 acres of land at Shiloh, although more has been added in recent years.

The park commission was most heavily involved in the story of the Battle of Shiloh, but it was also interested in other aspects of history. When it acquired the land on which several Indian mounds sat, it decided to excavate the burial mound in 1899, as seen here. The result was the discovery of several burials as well as the famous Shiloh funerary pipe.

Eventually, the park commission gained title to the vast majority of the battlefield, acquiring the famous sites such as Bloody Pond, the Peach Orchard, and the Hornet's Nest. This 1890s-era photograph shows the famous Sunken Road that ran through the Hornet's Nest, giving ample evidence that the road was not terribly sunken during the battle.

The park commission located additional historic sites outside the congressionally authorized boundaries of the park. One of these was Overshot Mill, between Shiloh and Adamsville, Tennessee, which had played a role in Lew Wallace's famous march to the Shiloh battlefield. The commission eventually located the entire route of Wallace's march with the help of Wallace himself and several of his officers.

Perhaps the most sacred spots on the battlefield were those special to the veterans who came back, especially those who worked there. Francis A. Large was the park's range rider or guard, and he had been captured near the Hornet's Nest on the first day of battle. Here, he poses on the exact spot of his capture.

While the engineers were mapping the battlefield and the land agents were buying the land, the commission concentrated on gathering items with which it would eventually mark the field. While Reed (right) developed the history, Cadle worked with the War Department to obtain antiquated cannon tubes and ordnance for use in monumenting the park. These arrived in 1897 but had to be stored until placed on the field.

While waiting on the land purchasing process to gain enough terrain so that the commission could legally place tablets, monuments, and cannons on the battlefield, the park managers decided to place very rudimentary signage to give the growing number of visitors something to see. Thus, in the early months of 1896, "before the spring excursion parties begin to arrive," the commission warned, these poplar boards painted white with red letters went up all over the battlefield, some 100 of them. They marked such places as the Johnston tree, the Hornet's Nest, and, as seen here, the Bloody Pond. It was the first systematic interpretive effort at Shiloh, and it would inadvertently play a major role in defining for the popular mindset the most important locations at Shiloh. Note the fence running through the pond denoting a land ownership boundary.

Eventually, the park commission acquired the necessary land and began to place more substantial cast-iron signage. Troop position tablets, artillery, and monuments all went up, as well as iron directional signs. This small tablet denotes Shiloh Spring, just south of the Shiloh Church, which was a favorite place of returning veterans.

The park commission also marked in more permanent fashion the burial places of the Confederate dead, those that could be located decades after the battle. Cornelius Cadle, Marcus Wright, James Ashcraft, and David Reed salute at a Southern burial trench. Note the modern signage as well as the American flags, a sign of the reconciliation of the times.

Because of some discord between the cemetery officials and the battlefield commission, the park authorities later moved their office to the hotel that sat just west of the cemetery, although there were still no permanent living accommodations. Nevertheless, the park progressed. Note the cannonballs and cannons waiting to be placed on the battlefield, while an Illinois artillery monument is already up.

Given the lack of accommodations in the early years of the park, the staff had to make the best of its living situations, often moving from place to place. Will Pride, one of the park's engineering laborers, is packed up and moving camp. Note the necessities of life: a rocking chair, bedding, and a rifle.

One of the first items on the agenda once the land became government property was to stabilize the crude roads in the area. This road crew with a roller is making the notoriously bad roads in the isolated Shiloh area fit for the thousands of visitors who were already converging on the battlefield.

Much of the road work was performed with manual labor and draft animals. Fortunately, the park itself was found to contain ample sources of rock, which was perfect for graveling roads. It was just a matter of getting it to where it was needed. Note the extent of the excavations.

This view shows the large operation of hauling gravel at Shiloh. The pick men to the left broke up the material, while the shovel men in the center loaded it onto the wagons. Then the drivers took their horse-drawn loads to the construction sites. It was a massive operation, but the park was fortunate that local gravel saved many miles of travel.

A different shot of the same process shows how deep the workers dug. Unfortunately, an accident occurred at one gravel pit in 1899, killing and injuring a number of workers. Although some of the pits were later landscaped, a few are still discernible deep in the woods on the park today.

Another view of the park laborers gives a sense of the great logistical effort it took to create acceptable roads at Shiloh National Military Park. The roads these workers created lasted into the 1930s and saw the transformation from horse-drawn transportation to automobiles. Obviously, newer and stronger materials were later needed.

While the road-making process was occurring, the park workforce also built bridges over several streams on the battlefield. The earliest bridges were wood, as seen in this photograph of a bridge across Shiloh Branch. Note also the emergence of tablets to mark troop positions, as this tablet is marking the line of Patrick Cleburne's brigade on April 6, 1862.

Eventually, the park commission invested in much stronger and nicer stone bridges. This one, seen carrying the load of a horse and buggy, is an illustrative example of many found on the park after the turn of the 20th century. Note also the lining of the creek with rock.

Another example of the new stone bridges emplaced at Shiloh, this one also has the attending rock lining of the creek bed to ease erosion. The commission took efforts also to beautify the bridges while keeping the military themes of the park. Note the cannonballs decorating the bridge.

As the park construction process moved along, the various states began to appoint monument commissions to erect memorials to their state's troops who had fought at Shiloh. The national commission, or at least Cadle and Reed, met each one and worked out plans for the construction and dedications. The Ohio commission poses with Cadle and Reed in the national cemetery.

Iowa's monument commission also met with Cadle and Reed and posed for a photograph in front of the hotel. Unfortunately, a nasty controversy erupted between the Iowans on the national commission, Cadle and Reed, the Iowa State Commission, and veterans over troop positions and timing. Neither side gave in, but the process went on fairly peaceably.

The Illinois state monument commission visited Shiloh to locate and mark the positions of its troops during the battle. Most of the time, the commission would visit, locate the most prominent position of each regiment or battery, and return to its state to design and build the monuments. Once created, the stone memorials would be sent to Shiloh, normally by boat, to be put in place on concrete foundations provided by the national park. Once all was done, each state held elaborate dedication ceremonies at the park. Often the state commissions contained famous generals, such as this photograph of the Illinois commission with John A. McClernand in the foreground pointing forward. Park commissioners and other staff are on the other end, including land agent J.W. Irwin, historian David D. Reed, engineer Atwell Thompson, commission chairman Cornelius Cadle, and Confederate commissioner Robert F. Looney.

Pennsylvania also sent a monument commission, as seen here near Pittsburg Landing. Pennsylvania had only one regiment in the battle but provided a very nice monument nevertheless. Although not a Pennsylvanian, famous general and author of *Ben Hur* Lew Wallace was also in attendance, sixth from the left. Wallace made several trips to the battlefield in an effort to rehabilitate his image, which was tarnished at Shiloh.

Illinois had more troops at Shiloh than any other state. It sent a commission to monument the battlefield and eventually erected a large state memorial as well as individual monuments to each unit. The commission posed while at Shiloh in front of the large stacks of cannonballs and cannons awaiting placement on the field.

While the state commissions concentrated on the monuments, the national commission, with historian Reed leading the way, marked the remainder of the battlefield with iron tablets denoting troop positions. He also marked campsites and artillery positions. The cannon tubes were placed on cast-iron carriages, marking where artillery was engaged. The rural landscape was not diminished, as seen in this photograph with cows in the foreground.

Another view of the rural battlefield shows the developing monumentation. Illinois unit monuments can be seen at right, while Ohio monuments are on the left. In the rear is the northern branch of the Methodist Episcopal church, which split with the southern branch over slavery prior to the war. This postwar church sat just a few hundred yards north of the more famous southern church, Shiloh Church.

One of the best Shiloh photographs for showing the developing park is this one, with the view looking eastward along the Hamburg-Purdy Road. The field at left is Review Field, so named because Union troops held reviews here in the days and weeks before the battle. Heavy action raged here during the battle itself. The 77th Pennsylvania Monument can be seen in the foreground, as well as a line of Indiana monuments to the right. Note the stone bridge in the foreground. In rear is "Review Place," which was the eventual home of the park's engineer, Atwell Thompson, once more land was obtained and better living facilities were acquired. Later, historian and then commission chairman David W. Reed, who moved from the north upon Thompson's resignation, lived here. Reed became the on-site director, living and directing the work of the park from here for many years.

When the park was established, the enabling legislation allowed the government to buy or condemn the locals' land, including any structures they lived in. Fortunately, the legislation allowed the locals to remain in their homes as tenants, paying a small rent. While some were upset at losing their homes and land, most went to work on the park as laborers and were glad to receive a steady income. This view illustrates the combining of historic monumentation and preexisting housing. A headquarters monument went up in Duncan Field near the Hornet's Nest and Sunken Road, which was the site of heavy fighting on both days of battle, while immediately in rear a residence continued to be used for decades. Eventually, park managers made the decision to stop the tenancy and chose to tear down the structures. Today, these house sites are most noticeable in the spring when flowers, which formally decorated yards, bloom seemingly in the middle of nowhere.

The park commission took great pains to keep the road network as historic as possible, although engineer Thompson, an Irish immigrant too young to be a veteran of the war, was less concerned about them than the veterans were. Over time, the roads were slightly altered, as this view of the crossings of Shiloh Branch attests. Today, the road and the tablets sit farther to the right.

By the second decade of the 20th century, this scene was becoming a rarity, not only at Pittsburg Landing, but also throughout the nation. With the rise of the automobile and increased mobility, more visitors began to visit the park, but by a different mode of transportation. A new era was emerging at Shiloh. (Courtesy of *Indiana at Shiloh*.)

Three

Memories in Stone and Bronze

Monuments of Shiloh

From its 1894 establishment as a federally preserved national military park, the landscape of Shiloh was to be managed in such a way as to allow states whose troops had participated in the battle to appoint commissions for the purpose of proposing, designing, and contracting for the placement of memorials or regimental monuments. The commission established guidelines for the protocol and material requirements in 1899, and by 1902, the monumentation of Shiloh was well underway.

As of 2012, 152 state and regimental monuments, headquarters, and mortuary and burial monuments adorn the 4,000-plus acre landscape. Visitors often revere the stone and bronze edifices as elaborate historical markers or as priceless works of art by America's noted sculptors. To the veterans of America's first monster battle, however, the statuary was much more. It embodied full representations of the brave soldiers of North and South and thus told the stories that they wished to convey to future generations.

To tell those stories, many monuments consisted of the most intricate detailing in bronze or stone. Even for elements impossible for viewing at ground level, details were paramount; the sculptures were seemingly prepared to come to life, step off of their bases, and continue the fight. Allegorical figures such as Fame or Liberty appear as they are pining to share the emotion conveyed in their lifelike expressions. Taken all together, Shiloh's monumentation is an impressive rendition of the battle as told by the veterans themselves.

For several years after the battle, the site of Gen. Albert Sidney Johnston's death was in dispute. In 1896, Isham G. Harris, Johnston's volunteer aide, former Tennessee governor, and now US senator, identified the area near this oak tree as the place where he found the mortally wounded general slumping in his saddle. Harris also identified an adjacent ravine 50 yards to the south as the location of Johnston's death. Based on Harris's information, the park commission posted this sign on an insignificant oak tree, giving rise to the legend of the "Johnston Tree." After the loss of the actual death tree in the nearby ravine, and despite a marker identifying the actual death location, this "Johnston Tree" became known as the tree under which the general had died.

The 9th Illinois Infantry lost 366 of its 578 men at Shiloh. This granite monument, honoring the regiment's dead and wounded, is the only battle-specific memorial in the national cemetery and was the first to go up on the battlefield. Dedicated in June 1896, the ceremony, attended by an estimated 5,000 onlookers, featured a patriotic band, more than a dozen unit veterans, and an address by Gen. Don Carlos Buell.

The commission placed square metal tablets on the battlefield to provide historic information or non-battle-specific details. Tablet rims were colored for easy identification: red for the Confederate Army of the Mississippi, blue for the Union Army of the Tennessee, and yellow for the Union Army of the Ohio. The commission placed a total of 651 tablets on the field: 171 Confederate, 226 Union, and 254 directional and informational signs.

The commission placed square metal tablets with ornamental corners to delineate unit locations on Shiloh's first day. Looking north across Shiloh Branch, these three red-trimmed tablets mark Confederate brigade positions that morning. The open terrain here resulted in many Confederate casualties. Shiloh Church sits about 200 yards beyond the trees to the right of this view.

Facing south into the heart of the Hornet's Nest, this yellow-trimmed oval tablet marks a second-day battle position. This open wood is representative of the mature forest landscape that was present at the time of the battle. A line of first-day markers and monuments to Hickenlooper's 5th Ohio Light Artillery and the 8th Iowa Infantry can be seen in the background along the Sunken Road.

Looking northeast up the Eastern Corinth Road, the David Wilson Reed family rests among red-trimmed first day tablets. These markers show locations of Confederate assaults against the famous Hornet's Nest. What caused great difficulty for advancing Confederate soldiers was not the later-named Sunken Road, but an "impenetrable thicket" of briars and undergrowth that formed a natural defensive barrier.

This mortuary monument marking Union general W.H.L. Wallace's wounding was completed in 1902. These monuments marked where officers of brigade level and above fell. The War Department specified that battlefield monuments, intended to last in perpetuity, be made of bronze, granite, or marble. Seeking a cheaper alternative, the federal government exercised a clause allowing for the use of "similar durable stone." Five mortuary and 13 headquarters monuments of unreinforced concrete and iron cannons and projectiles were thus erected.

The most famous of the five mortuary monuments at Shiloh commemorates the area of Albert Sidney Johnston's wounding and death, although over the years, controversy and confusion have developed over the various sites. Johnston was actually wounded in Sarah Bell's cotton field across the road from this monument, but he rode to this prominent knoll to view the effects of the charge he had just led. It was here that Tennessee governor Isham G. Harris found the wounded Johnston already suffering from a loss of blood. Harris then took Johnston to the ravine in the rear, where he actually died. Thus, the monument marks neither the site of his wounding nor his death but rather the place where Harris found the wounded general. Over time, however, mainly because the park commission marked the famous tree in background, this knoll and the tree became known as Johnston's death site.

Shortly after completion, the mortuary monument to W.H.L. Wallace received an elaborate surround. This ornamentation and stairway were later removed, probably due to rapid deterioration of the unreinforced concrete. (Courtesy of *Dedication of Monuments to Iowa Soldiers*.)

In 1902 and 1903, the commission placed 13 monuments on the battlefield to mark the locations of Union division and brigade headquarters during the weeks prior to the battle. This monument marks the headquarters of Brig. Gen. John McArthur, commander of the 2nd Brigade of W.H.L. Wallace's 2nd Division, Army of the Tennessee.

This monument, a short distance north of Shiloh Church, marks the divisional headquarters of Brig. Gen. William T. Sherman. The exact location was derived from witness recollections, maps, and a tree felled at the site in 1895 with "Sherman" inscribed on its bark. Headquarters monuments came in two sizes, with division monuments being considerably larger than brigade monuments.

At the urging of the War Department, the national military parks sent a sample of their work to various fairs held across the nation. This photograph shows the Shiloh exhibit at the 1904 St. Louis Louisiana Purchase Exposition. Neither the Shiloh commission nor the other battlefields' directors were enthused about sending their precious items away from the battlefields.

Workers pause after transporting the 6th Ohio Infantry monument up the steep incline from Pittsburg Landing. While river transportation was the most cost-effective way to transport the monuments to the remote battlefield, specially configured wagons and large draft horses were required to pull the massive granite monuments up the hill from the river and across the battlefield.

Ohio placed 34 granite monuments on the battlefield to honor its 28 infantry, one cavalry, and five artillery units at Shiloh. Most are of unique design, such as this one for the 54th Ohio Infantry. The regiment's monument accurately depicts a common soldier in his French-influenced Zouave uniform.

This unique monument along the Sunken Road marks the earnest and brave stand of Capt. Andrew Hickenlooper's 5th Ohio Light Artillery. Located in the center of the Hornet's Nest, the battery's guns repulsed repeated Confederate attacks on the Union position that day. Unfortunately, the polished granite cannon tube disappeared many decades ago.

The state monument commissions placed most regimental monuments where a unit made its greatest contribution during the battle. This monument to the 77th Ohio Infantry sits on the high ground just south of Shiloh Church, which is visible in the background, and is 50 yards in front of the camp where it met the heavy Confederate assault on April 6. (Courtesy of *Ohio at Shiloh*.)

On the 41st anniversary of the battle on April 6 and 7, 1903, Indiana veterans and their families dedicated 22 recently placed limestone obelisks. Twenty of these represented infantry units and displayed crossed rifles, a cartridge box, and a canteen in bas-relief. A single artillery monument, seen here, displayed crossed cannons, and the one cavalry monument featured crossed sabers in their scabbards. (Courtesy of *Indiana at Shiloh*.)

The 77th Pennsylvania Infantry was the only eastern regiment to fight at Shiloh and was the first to be represented on the battlefield in bronze. Dedicated in November 1903, the monument features an ornate granite pedestal supporting a life-sized bronze infantryman, uniformed and equipped like the soldiers in 1862. The $10,000 monument is a classic example of monuments placed on courthouse squares throughout the North and South. (Courtesy of *Seventy-Seventh Pennsylvania at Shiloh*.)

Artist Richard Bock created the Illinois State Monument, located near some of Shiloh's most intense fighting in Wolfe Field. Costing $65,000 and dedicated in 1904 to all Illinois participants in the battle, the motherly figure has many significant details not visible from the ground. Bock modeled Liberty after his wife, of whom he made a plaster cast shortly after she gave birth. She holds a book of Illinois history in her wedding-ring-adorned left hand, her middle finger placed as a marker at the state's sacrifices on April 6 and 7, 1862. In her right hand is an intricately detailed sheathed sword, the protective mother remaining armed and ever prepared. Sitting in her throne, she remains cautious, keeping watch toward enemy territory to the south. A bronze relief on the front of the granite base features a scene of intense combat. One model for the relief was a young man named Joseph Liebchen, who became a well-known silent movie actor during the 1910s, Stuart Holmes. (Courtesy of *Wisconsin at Shiloh*.)

Though Shiloh's federally improved roads were vastly superior to those off of the park grounds, the commission took great care to use techniques that would incur as little damage as possible. Teams of oxen or draft horses were the norm, with wagon wheel widths being determined in correlation with the gross weight of the monument being moved. In this photograph, a team of 10 oxen transports a stocky but heavy Illinois regimental monument past the national cemetery.

Illinois placed 40 monuments across the field. Each granite monument was nearly identical in shape, with the respective unit designation inscribed on the front. A bronze tablet affixed to the back provided detail of the unit's contributions and accomplishments in the battle. Here, the monument to Battery D, 1st Illinois Light Artillery marks activity in Review Field, located in the heart of the park.

The heavily forested nature of the Shiloh battlefield limited the use of cavalry in organized combat. Cavalry served in a variety of other roles, such as division headquarters guards and special escorts. This monument to Illinois's cavalry consists of a six-sided granite body with conical top. A bronze plaque on each face provides battle details for each unit. (Courtesy of *Illinois at Shiloh*.)

Dedicated on August 22, 1905, the 2nd Tennessee Infantry monument was the first Confederate memorial placed on the field. The detail of the slightly larger-than-life soldier is impeccable, with the hammer on his musket at full cock, indicating that he is ever prepared. The location, just southeast of Shiloh Church, was the scene of intense fighting involving this and other Confederate units.

The State of Wisconsin dedicated its elaborate monument on April 7, 1906. The main bronze features an allegorical figure of Victory holding a flag with its staff shattered. She is supporting a fallen color sergeant, who holds his mortal wound near his heart as if to stay off death long enough to see the battle won.

The dedication of the Wisconsin State monument was very typical of those that occurred during Shiloh's veteran commemoration period. The Savannah Military Band entertained the audience with patriotic music, followed by the governor of Wisconsin transferring ownership of monuments to the US government. The program continued with emotive orations from both Union and Confederate military leaders. (Courtesy of *Wisconsin at Shiloh*.)

Numerous annual reunions allowed Shiloh veterans to take succeeding generations of family members to battlefield locations that changed their lives. Gatherings, such as this one of Wisconsin veterans around 1906, were an opportunity for survivors to not only share their stories but also to strike up new friendships with former foes. (Courtesy of *Wisconsin at Shiloh*.)

Designed by F.R. Triebel and dedicated in 1906, the 75-foot tall Iowa State monument towers above all others on the battlefield. The fluted shaft is topped by a bronze capital, globe, and eagle. The eagle's wings spread 15 feet from tip to tip. Ascending the steps at the monument's base is an allegorical statue of Fame, inscribing a tribute of homage in the granite. (Courtesy of *Dedication of Monuments to Iowa Soldiers*.)

Iowa, like Illinois, placed monuments of an identical design on the Shiloh battlefield, differing only in respective text. Eleven granite and bronze monuments went up at sites of significant unit participation. A bronze state seal graced the front of each, while bronze laurel wreaths of peace decorated both sides. A large bronze interpretive panel adorned the back.

The State of Alabama placed an impressive monument to its troops on the battlefield in 1907. The second Confederate monument erected in the park, this memorial witnessed a small delegation of hardy representatives attending the dedication on a wet May day. The monument was among the first to be funded by donations from the general public and schoolchildren rather than by state funds. The United Daughters of the Confederacy coordinated the effort. (Courtesy of Jeff Wilkes.)

Munch's Battery, 1st Minnesota Artillery, was the only Minnesota unit at Shiloh. This unit held steadfast in the Union center of the Hornet's Nest as Confederates attempted to crush the stronghold on the first day. No stranger to the design of military statuary, St. Paul artist John K. Daniels created a life-size depiction of a young, resolute Minnesota artilleryman. The soldier looks westward across the Sunken Road and out over Duncan Field, watching for the next Confederate assault. Though in actual combat, an artilleryman would never remove his protective clothing, doing such for this representation, fists clenched and veins bulging, emphasizes the determination and defiance of the men of Munch's battery. The monument, dedicated in April 1908, was widely praised for its representation of the common soldier.

Erected by the federal government itself, monuments to the US Regulars also went up on the field of Shiloh. Batteries from the 4th and 5th US Artillery held this position north of the Bloody Pond on the second day of combat. D.W. Reed is seen in back.

Though the majority of infantry regiments fighting in the west were state units, US Regulars fought with great success as well. During the Battle of Shiloh, portions of the 15th, 16th, and 19th Regular US Infantries served with Buell's Army of the Ohio, participating in the second day of combat. This monument marks the Regulars' position, supporting the far right flank of the Union line at the Hornet's Nest.

The efforts of the Arkansas chapters of the United Daughters of the Confederacy resulted in the 1911 placement of a monument to that state's Shiloh troops. Costing $15,000, the 40-foot-high granite pilaster is topped by a life-size granite soldier. Located in the heart of the Hornet's Nest, the soldier is seen peering through the smoke of battle toward the enemy line.

As the years passed, fewer and fewer veterans were able to attend reunions and dedications. Concurrently, World War I and its sacrifices overshadowed attention to the feats of Civil War veterans. The May 1919 dedication of the Michigan State monument marked the last placement to occur for several decades. (Courtesy of *Michigan at Shiloh*.)

Located near large population centers served by better transportation systems, battlefields such as Gettysburg, Chickamauga, and Vicksburg tended to receive more large-scale monuments and sizable commemorative investments than Shiloh. National efforts on the part of the United Daughters of the Confederacy changed that trend with the placement of a monument to all Shiloh Confederate soldiers that rivaled those of other battlefields. Designed and built by artist Fredrick Hibbard, a student of Lorado Taft, the Shiloh monument garnered nationwide praise. The May 17, 1917, dedication was the largest in Shiloh National Military Park history, with an estimated 15,000 people attending the grand unveiling. (Courtesy of John Ross.)

The design of the Confederate Monument personifies the tradition of the Southern "Lost Cause." Its location marks the Confederate "high-water mark" where, on the afternoon of April 6, Confederate forces encircled and captured 2,200 Union troops, ending the daylong stand at the Hornet's Nest. The monument's central bronze figures depict Defeated Victory. In the front, the South surrenders the laurel wreath of victory to Death on her right and Night on her left. Death took away Gen. Albert Sidney Johnston, and night allowed for Union reinforcement. Below the figures in low relief is an image of Johnston, who remains the highest-ranking American officer ever to die in battle. On the right, the infantryman snatches up the Confederate flag in defiance, while his colleague, artillery, gazes through the smoke of battle toward Pittsburg Landing. To the far left, the cavalryman expresses frustration at that branch's limitations due to the thick forest of Shiloh. Lastly, the Confederate officer holds his head bowed in submission to orders to cease firing on the night of April 6, when Southern victory had appeared imminent. (Courtesy of John Ross.)

Following a closing benediction, Shiloh's largest ever peacetime gathering came to an end. Though dramatically honoring the Confederate soldiers of Shiloh, orations at the dedication strongly encouraged reconciliation, not division. (Courtesy of John Ross.)

Funding for the $50,000 memorial came by donations from all corners of the United States. The Shiloh monument was revered as a befitting honor not only to the Confederacy at Shiloh but also to Southerners nationwide. Commemorative wreaths from various United Daughters of the Confederacy chapters adorned the monument. (Courtesy of John Ross.)

Landscape work continued following the dedication. Better roads leading to the military park provided for greater automobile access, resulting in improvements to accommodate more traffic. A wide, circular drive went around the Confederate monument, allowing for vehicle access to the tablets affixed to the structure's back wall. In time, such early and perhaps excessive improvements were removed, park management in later decades preferring to keep as much of the park in as natural a setting as possible. (Courtesy of *Michigan at Shiloh*.)

Four

Tragedy Turned Opportunity

The Cyclone of 1909

"At 5:26 p.m., a cyclone visited the park." Those words introduced the October 14, 1909, entry in the *Daily Events* ledger book of the Shiloh National Military Park Commission. The devastation left by the sudden storm was almost indescribable. Even the dozen or so photographs recording the event fail to fully illustrate the damage to what had been the nucleus of park development and veteran reunification.

The violent storm struck Pittsburg Landing and the national cemetery at sunset on October 14. Residents said that the weather throughout the day had been of peculiar imbalance. Despite such conditions, daily activities in and around the landing had gone on as normal until black clouds formed to the north and "clouds were seen to clash, boil together, spew with electricity, suddenly fall, rapidly whirl." Within moments, the buildings, landscape, and livelihood of the small hamlet of Pittsburg Landing were forever changed, and, most unfortunately, seven residents were killed and 33 were injured.

Park staff and area residents worked throughout the night rescuing and treating the injured. When morning came, survivors saw for the first time the enormity of the devastation. What wind had not leveled, fire completed the task of destruction, including the hotel.

The destruction to federal property was greater than the park staff or base funding could address. Plans for future development were thus put on hold and all attention diverted to reconstruction. Congress quickly responded, allocating $8,000 for the national cemetery and $19,500 for the military park. Area residents were not so blessed by immediate funding, many starting their lives over from scratch.

Within seconds, the storm leveled the warehouse at Pittsburg Landing, as well as the stables, sheds, and most of the other structures that were associated with the national cemetery. Only the heavily damaged cemetery superintendent's office and house remained standing. The residence was found to be too unstable to be saved, and it was later razed.

The cemetery house was of the standard design in almost all early national cemeteries. Designed by Quartermaster General Montgomery Meigs, the houses were in the popular mansard roof style and of substantial brick construction for pleasing appearance, practicality, and durability. However, even the most durable construction proved unequal to the October storm.

Capt. George Dean, national cemetery superintendent, reported, "Mrs. Dean and I were sitting in the office, and she remarked 'what is that roaring?' We went to the window and saw the cloud coming. . . . About that time, I saw the lodge in the yard rise and seemed to melt away. The glass begin [*sic*] to strike my face and I left the window, and the room seemed to spin around like a top. When I came to myself, everything was gone out of the office but desk and relic case and typewriter. The wall was gone, and the door was gone."

Winds propelled trees and structural debris several hundred feet and spread personal belongings over tens of miles. The magnitude of the damage is almost unfathomable, but fortunately a Corinth photographer, J.E. France, provided a historic record of the destruction.

Massive trees that had survived countless winds and storms were tossed about the Pittsburg Landing area. Many cemetery trees that witnessed the battle, including the ivy-covered oak that Grant rested under the night of April 6, 1862, were destroyed. Marble grave markers placed into the earth to a depth of almost three feet were tilted, snapped at ground level, or in some cases pulled right out of the ground.

Serving for decades as the centerpiece of veteran reunions, orations, and special services, the national cemetery rostrum was totally demolished. Laborers later found remnants of the decorative cast-iron structure strewn along the cemetery terrace, but portions of the structure were later put to other uses. The iron staircase and banister that provided access to the structure have long served as the entry steps to the southeastern corner of the cemetery.

The enormous 1860s dedication monument, consisting of a Columbiad cannon tube mounted vertically in stone, proved the one structure able to withstand the impact of the wind and debris. Trees nearby are seen uprooted and others are seen sheered off near the top. Amazingly, ornamental bushes, visible in the far background, appear relatively unscathed.

Total devastation is visible near the hamlet of Pittsburg Landing. Storm survivor Thomas Lewis recollected, "When I managed to make my way out of the debris I began to wander, but it was so dark and everything was so changed that I could scarcely find where my cottage stood." The next morning, searching for belongings proved difficult on the flattened landscape.

Neighbors immediately began helping neighbors. Since virtually every structure in the Pittsburg Landing area was destroyed or damaged beyond use, residents farther out on the park opened their homes for shelter. Shiloh Commission secretary and historian David W. Reed and his wife opened their undamaged home a mile and a half southwest of the devastation to the injured.

"We found our barn, two tenant houses, orchard fences, etc., all gone, the damage will amount to about $800 or $1,000. The assistance of the good people was given us, for which we are thankful and appreciative," said Mrs. Bell.

Locating loved ones was, for most, an emotional task. "I began calling for my children and each of the three youngest began answering, 'Here I am, mamma.' Oh! How this made my heart leap with joy. Soon we began releasing ourselves from under the debris. . . . I felt so thankful that all of us had not perished," reported Mrs. W.P. Littlefield.

The greatest damage to US government property was the loss of items key to the research and development of the park. Cornelius Cadle expressed sadness over the loss of "all the records, notes or surveys, maps, original drawings, orders, correspondence, supplies, heavy furniture, office desks with roll tops (2), large table, office chairs, file cases, library of 300 volumes, stove, valuable relics, everything has disappeared completely."

While virtually everything of use was either destroyed or simply gone, park employees were able to recover some useful material. The vital blacksmith shop was found intact, though shifted on its foundation. The workshop that stored tools and equipment was blown over, protecting much of the property inside. Miraculously, some of the park animals that were trapped in debris survived.

The pyramidal roof of the cemetery well can be seen behind the gentleman on the left. The tents of the Shiloh Commission were located to the left of the well. Despite significant challenges for management of the national cemetery and the national military park, opportunity for the future was soon realized. The need for replacement buildings, design, and equipment opened the door to opportunity for more efficient operations and facilities for the cemetery and the park.

The destruction in and around the national cemetery was extensive. For areas west of Pittsburg Landing, the most noticeable damage was the toppling of the relatively new Iowa State Monument. The massive fluted column separated at its base, falling due east, severing the extended left arm of Fame and damaging the stones below.

The scale of the Iowa State Monument is evident by viewing the woman standing at the far right end of the felled granite column and the young girl sitting atop it. As part of its post-storm assistance, Congress appropriated $15,000 for the repair of the monument, with the understanding that Iowa would fully reimburse the federal government.

Five

A New Generation
Shiloh in the Post-Veteran Era

The loss of property and infrastructure in the cyclone was devastating to the maturing military park and its adjacent cemetery. Yet out of the proverbial ashes, a new and better Pittsburg Landing arose. Starting largely with a clean slate on which to build, the commission took great care to ensure that the replacement structures corrected many of the deficiencies that had plagued earlier operations. Within two years, the majority of the landing's needs were reconstructed, and new lodges, offices, out buildings, a hotel, and a store greeted visitors. The commission and the states also repaired or replaced damaged monuments and made improvements to the surrounding landscape.

But the renewal at Pittsburg Landing was not the only change during this time. Aging members of the park commission were passing away, and the inevitable end soon came to the government's practice of veteran-only management. The new manager, DeLong Rice, a poet, orator, and thespian, proved in some respects quite unconventional when compared to the veteran management of the previous 20 years. Rice realized that the traditional tourist demographic was changing, and new interpretation and ideas were needed. He enhanced trail access to isolated monuments and created publications and signage to guide visitors who were not nearly as versed in military experience as the veterans. Trained, licensed guides told the park-directed story in a manner understandable to all ages and backgrounds.

Still, while many developmental changes occurred during this period, the traditional battlefield interpretation, especially the official story established by the late D.W. Reed, nonetheless remained paramount, and the hard work and desire of the original Shiloh management continued.

Cleanup by the park's workforce began the day after the storm. Though consisting of fewer than two dozen workers, the laborers removed most of the debris and some of the estimated 10,000 downed trees within weeks. Many of those trees were milled on-site and used to rebuild barns and other necessary structures. Within 10 months, all destroyed park buildings, with the exception of park offices and accommodations, had been replaced.

Reconstruction in the national cemetery moved slightly slower than that in the park. In many ways, it was a more difficult undertaking. The entire cemetery was redesigned, with workers straightening, repairing, or replacing headstones as appropriate. Also, a new gambrel-roofed cemetery office and residence went up just to the north of the former building sites. On the west side, a decorative concrete wall with iron ornamental gates went up in 1911.

The commission undertook careful planning to ensure that a replacement park office was of adequate space and design for workers and quarters. The boilerplate War Department design was a major improvement from the small size of the former hotel, and emergency funding and later appropriations funded the project in January 1911. In this photograph, the new building is complete with orientation tablets and an ornate iron gate. The post-storm national cemetery wall and house are to the right.

A new store and a hotel were situated at the landing by the end of 1910. In this photograph, from left to right, are the new hotel, park headquarters, a new store, and park shops. The present-day visitor center sits in the middle ground of the field to the left. The present-day park bookstore sits on the site of the 1910 headquarters.

DeLong Rice arrived at Shiloh in May 1913 as park secretary. With the death of the last of the Shiloh Commission members, Rice was soon promoted to the position of park director. Preferring the title "superintendent," the flamboyant son of a Confederate veteran viewed the park, its resources, and story with new eyes and a keen awareness of changing visitor demographics. Rice modernized the park in many ways and brought the story of Shiloh to new generations of audiences. (Courtesy of *Michigan at Shiloh*.)

Rice expanded construction efforts at Shiloh, focusing on appearance and visitor understanding. Yet he held firm to Reed's interpretive basis for Shiloh—promoting the overemphasized legacy of the Hornet's Nest, the Sunken Road, and Bloody Pond. To his credit, Rice developed hiking and automobile trails, with tour stops keyed to specific points of interest. Some improvements were more imposing, like the natural Bloody Pond fully concreted and encircled by the iron fence seen in this photograph.

During the 1920s, park improvements included trail construction to key points of interest and monuments. In this photograph is the trail leading from the Gen. Albert Sidney Johnston mortuary monument to the tree under which he died. Despite the improved trail and park interpretive maps directing visitors to the death site, most visitors, as is true today, never ventured to the correct site, perpetuating instead the "Johnston Tree" myth.

Rice was convinced that a hotel was in order at Shiloh. Located southwest of the park boundary, the Pine Lodge Hotel was comparable to hotel structures in the great national parks of the west. Built of pine logs and native stone, the hotel had opulent accommodations, swimming pools, and tennis courts. Rice sold shares in the enterprise, providing lots in exchange for investment money. The grand structure was a fiscal failure, and it burned down in the 1980s.

Completed in 1918, the pine-log superintendent's residence featured beautifully hewn interior timbers and side porches supported by vertically mounted artillery tubes. An impressive showpiece for Rice's park development scheme, this trophy became a place of tragedy in September 1929, when an acetylene gas explosion in the home fatally injured DeLong Rice and his 16-year-old son James. With Rice's passing, another chapter of Shiloh leadership came to an end.

Perhaps Rice's greatest triumph as superintendent was the federal acquisition of a turnpike between Corinth, Mississippi, and Shiloh National Military Park. Closely following the historic 1862 road, visitors approaching the park from the south entered through large stone pilasters fitted with prominent bronze plaques. Capitalizing on this busy entrance, a small community fittingly named Shiloh emerged, providing services once available at Pittsburg Landing. No longer did the majority of visitors arrive at the battlefield by packet boat. Road improvements and the popularity of the automobile changed how visitors experienced the park, and the burgeoning Shiloh community was there to provide accommodations, a store, restaurants, and fuel.

Two decades after the 1909 cyclone, the devastation at Pittsburg Landing was only a memory. Trees planted as replacements for the lost specimens ravaged by the wind were now mature and healthy. Dense ivy securely grew on the sides of the park headquarters building and the nearby national cemetery lodge. The automobile was becoming the primary method for touring, and Shiloh's macadamized roads provided some of the smoothest surfaces in the region.

This photograph, taken from the second story of the park headquarters building, provides an impressive example of the many special annual events at Pittsburg Landing. In addition to veteran and patriotic observances, concerts, special lectures, and cooperative association meetings made use of the 40-by-120-foot pavilion in the background.

As was customary at each Memorial Day exercise, Civil War veterans displayed their fife and drum talents at Pittsburg Landing. Taken around 1918, this photograph shows 14-year-old Dixie Donald, to the right with hands in pocket, who was born and raised on the Shiloh National Military Park. His family was among the first of the licensed tour guides on the grounds. (Courtesy of Dixie Decker.)

DeLong Rice placed great emphasis on ensuring that battle interpretation was understandable not only to the veterans but also for the following generations. Passing a relatively thorough exam, largely based upon Reed's emphasis on the Hornet's Nest and Sunken Road thesis, was required prior to licensure. A lifelong Shiloh resident and a Confederate veteran, Lynn Surratt served for many years as an official guide.

In the years following the 1862 battle, informal tours of the battlefield by wagon or buggy were available. These tours carried on well into the early years of park development. As with the advent of licensed guides, services also improved with the use of horse-drawn "buses" that took visitors from the landing to key points on the park. One local guide, Wilds Donnell, provided countless informative bus tours. (Courtesy of Jeff Wilkes.)

During the early decades of the 20th century, ornate fences were a favorite of the park administration. Rhea Springs, south of Shiloh Church, is a series of natural springs along the Shiloh Branch. The attractive location was a site for reunions, picnics, and weddings. Restored to a natural battle-period setting, the springs remain a popular location for picnics and nuptials today.

An early park acquisition was a small store that served the Pittsburg Landing community and early visitors to the battlefield and national cemetery. The original structure was destroyed in the 1909 cyclone, and this building took its place in 1910. The mercantile continued to be run as a concession in this building until 1936, when it was replaced by a CCC-built structure.

It was not until 1881 that a frame replacement for the original log Shiloh Church was completed. The structure in this image is likely a third church, or the second church altered. Legend tells that the second church either burned or was heavily damaged in the 1909 cyclone. Funding for the Shiloh school (left) was raised in a variety of ways, including providing wagon tours to park visitors.

Needing a new sanctuary, the frame church was razed and work began on a new stone structure. Park Supt. DeLong Rice was a strong supporter of the project, but his death in 1929, combined with the onset of the Great Depression, halted building with the rough rock walls only a few feet in height. The congregation held services in the adjacent school until the new church was finished in 1948.

During the first quarter of the 20th century, many proposals for additions or changes to the battlefield park emerged, including a proposal for creating a large lake south of Shiloh Church. This image, depicting a proposed "memorial college" at Pittsburg Landing, is one of great mystery. There is no information found thus far regarding this substantial proposition that never became a reality. (Courtesy of Brian K. McCutchen.)

Six

Depression, War, and Change

Shiloh's Forward Progress

Shiloh National Military Park's history took another drastic turn in 1933, when jurisdiction over the Civil War battlefields went from the War Department to the National Park Service of the Interior Department. The change was reflected in many visual adjustments, such as uniformed personnel and regularly scheduled interpretative tours. There were also less noticeable changes as well, including those in administration, funding, and the massive paperwork required by the new governing agency.

Perhaps most significantly, the change from the War Department to the National Park Service reflected a larger transformation from the veteran generation's dominance at Shiloh to that of nonveterans. The 1920s had seen some nonveterans such as DeLong Rice emerge, but they had always held the veterans and their ideals very dear. They were, after all, trained by the men who had fought there. But the National Park Service, although patriotism and honor were no doubt very present, seemed more businesslike, focusing on management rather than personal care and interpretation rather than commemoration. This change reflected what was occurring in America itself.

The advent of the National Park Service at Shiloh corresponded with other national-level efforts, such as the New Deal. Shiloh would see massive amounts of money spent on the park through the mediums of the Civilian Conservation Corps, Civil Works Administration, Works Progress Administration, and Bureau of Public Roads. The face-lift that took place was second only to the initial phase of construction when the park was established.

Over time, as the Great Depression and World War II faded into memory, the National Park Service continued its task of preservation, interpretation, and education through up-to-date policies, renovations, living history, and media, most notably the 1956 narrative film *Shiloh: Portrait of a Battle*. The post-1933 Shiloh was vastly different from that of the commission era, but it still held the bloody Battle of Shiloh as the central story of its existence.

One of the most visible and productive of all New Deal agencies at Shiloh National Military Park was the Civilian Conservation Corps, better known as the CCC. Two camps operated on the park, with one located at Corinth, working on the government road between Shiloh and Corinth. The park had acquired the road in 1924, and the men performed maintenance and erosion control work on the thoroughfare. The other camp, pictured here, lived on the park itself and performed various jobs around the battlefield such as erosion control, construction, and maintenance. The camp enrollees were officially known as Company 2425, or Camp Young. Both CCC camps were made up of African American World War I veterans, who were not the standard young, white enrollees most CCC camps held. Note the white officers who commanded the African Americans in the days of segregation.

Much of the labor of both CCC camps involved road work. Here CCC laborers work on the main Corinth-to-Shiloh road just south of the park. Much of the work was actually on the shoulders of the roads, beautifying the landscape, checking erosion, and clearing site lines. While the CCC laborers had automobiles, they still performed some of their work with draft animals, as evidenced in this photograph.

CCC laborers also provided erosion control on the Tennessee River. The Tennessee Valley Authority's work on the river in creating dams and providing better transportation resulted in heavier barge traffic and higher water, which eroded the river bank faster than before. This group of CCC laborers is unloading rock to stabilize the bank.

Another major job of the CCC workers was to build stone walls at various places throughout the park. Trails, parking lots, and other areas gained beautiful stone walls, and most are still in use at the park today. This team of CCC stone masons is building one of the park's rock features.

Other New Deal agencies were at work on the park during the 1930s as well. Here, CCC workers are filling in one of the Indian mounds excavated in 1934 by Civilian Works Administration personnel under Smithsonian Institution supervision.

For decades after the battle, the local farmers in the area had continued working their land, but they knew very little of the modern ways to combat erosion, such as terracing. The CCC taught locals how to preserve their land and worked to reclaim what was already eroded. One of the worst eroded areas was Fraley Field, where the battle had begun. This is a check dam to stop further erosion.

The CCC enrollees lived in a camp near Shiloh Branch that included several barracks as well as other buildings. The former veterans were used to the semi-military format of the CCC. This is a flag raising ceremony in the CCC camp at Shiloh. Note the white officers in charge.

The extensive CCC camp at Shiloh National Military Park was a comfortable setting for the enrollees. This view shows the four barracks at left, with the central assembly area, as well as other buildings. The laborers made this camp their home for several years, but unfortunately, little is left of the camp today.

The CCC laborers were mainly at Shiloh to work, and they had a well-stocked supply of trucks and other equipment at their disposal. The enrollees are gathered here for their morning trek to the work sites. As with government agencies today, safety was a major concern, as evidenced by the fire prevention equipment.

The CCC enrollees had ample spare time for recreation. They could spend some of their money made on the job, although much of it went home to their families. They also had the opportunity to get an education or learn crafts. Here, several enrollees train a pet dog. The camp also had a goat as a mascot.

Part of the CCC effort was also community relations, and the men traveled all over the region doing community service. The semi-military structure of the CCC camp is evident as enrollees participate in a parade in Corinth, led by their white officer. The camp band played martial music, and even the camp's goat participated.

Other agencies besides the CCC were also hard at work at Shiloh National Military Park. The Works Progress Administration funded the construction of several new buildings at the park. A new visitor center, actually the first building in the park's history that was dedicated to visitor accommodation, was completed in 1935. It still serves as the visitor center today.

The WPA also funded other buildings, such as staff housing, entrance stations, and a concessions building, seen here. This small building sits across the road from the visitor center, on the site of the old administration building. It housed the park store as well as the post office for many years. Today, it is the park bookstore.

The New Deal also provided stations at the main entrances to the park. One sat on the road from the south entrance, and another went up at the western entrance. Completed in 1935, these small buildings allowed staff to welcome and orient visitors as they came into the park. Today, the stations are long gone, although the foundation for the one at the south entrance still exists.

The Bureau of Public Roads performed a lot of work at Shiloh. It oversaw the asphalting of secondary roads and the concreting of the main roads in the park in 1936. Pictured here is a view of Highway 22, the main road into the park from the south, with its nice concrete surfacing. In the distance the entrance station can be seen.

Overseeing all the early work of the New Deal agencies at Shiloh was park superintendent Robert A. Livingston. He had been a clerk at the park for years, was a World War I veteran, and took charge of the battlefield when DeLong Rice was killed. Unfortunately, Livingston did not survive a heated encounter with US Senator Kenneth McKellar, costing him his job in 1936.

Few superintendents in the ensuing years had as much of an impact as Livingston, but Ira B. Lykes certainly did. He revamped the park's interpretation in the 1950s, most notably with a new film, *Shiloh: Portrait of a Battle*. With historian Charles Shedd, Lykes created the film that became the park service's longest running film ever. Here, Lykes (left) and Shedd are seen with their creation.

Filming for the monumental production, which blazed the trail for other parks in moving from slide presentations to motion pictures, took place with park staff and volunteers in 1955. Here, the staff is seen filming the opening scenes of the bombardment of Fort Sumter. The film was first played on the battle's anniversary in 1956 and was only replaced in April 2012, the 150th anniversary of Shiloh.

Ira Lykes (left) was a military veteran as well as a gifted artist. While Shedd wrote the script, Lykes painted the maps used in the film and fashioned models of forts and gunboats. Here, he is seen with maintenance foreman J.B. Jordan working with the models of the *Tyler* and *Lexington*.

As the National Park Service entered a more modern phase of interpretation and education, managers followed through with Lykes's revolutionary approaches at Shiloh. But the interpretation never left its roots created under the original commission. Here, a ranger gives an introductory talk to a group of visitors inside the visitor center using the battle maps drawn by Atwell Thompson and David W. Reed half a century before.

Tours of the battlefield have always been a stalwart at Shiloh, from commission days up through the National Park Service years. Here, a guide gives visitors an interpretive talk on the national cemetery at the Ulysses S. Grant headquarters monument. The novel memorial had been erected in 1914 to replace the original tree, destroyed in 1909.

Through the years, there have been numerous approaches to interpreting the park and its historic sites, from hikes to stationary talks to bus tours. Park rangers also led tourists around the battlefield in car caravan tours. In order to tell the story efficiently and plainly, Shiloh rangers used a lead automobile fitted with loudspeakers. This tour is winding its way through the center of the park while the ranger in the lead vehicle tells the story of the battle. Barely visible at right is the cast-iron sign that denotes the Hornet's Nest, while the top of the Minnesota monument is visible above the cars.

Bus tours were also a popular means of interpreting the events of Shiloh. At least eight buses are lined up in front of the heavily shaded visitor center, which can be seen at right. The Iowa monument rises in the distance on the left. The circular drive in front of the visitor center no longer exists.

National Park Service rangers and licensed guides led walking tours of many of the park's historic places. In particular, Shiloh's monumentation was an early favorite topic of visitors. In this photograph, a guide is telling a crowd about the Wisconsin State Memorial in the Hornet's Nest.

Visitors took special interest in battle-aged relics as time passed and original structures and artifacts that dated to the battle became uncommon. This couple posed in front of the William Manse George war cabin near the Peach Orchard. Although not in terribly great shape even then, it was in much better condition under the National Park Service than when the original commission had taken over its care in the 1890s.

As part of the National Park Service's Mission 66 program of renewal, Shiloh gained some new features through the years. In addition to a bypass that took traffic out of the heart of the park, Shiloh also received new signage. This entrance sign on the new bypass welcomed visitors to the park.

Shiloh National Military Park also received new signage to easily and conveniently guide visitors around the battlefield. The first interpretive tour route came about in the 1920s under DeLong Rice, and the National Park Service built on that idea through the years. Over time, the emphasis went from monuments, so beloved by the veterans and the generation who placed them, to the historic physical features of the battlefield. These new additions are a numbered tour route sign as well as an interpretive marker with text and a map denoting the tent hospital site in the southeastern portion of the park. Here, Union doctors had cared for many of the wounded, saving numerous lives. But the new features are still shadowed by the old, including a rail fence for aesthetic purposes as well as one of the original monuments placed in the early 1900s by the State of Ohio. This monument denotes a position of the 71st Ohio at the battle.

Under the National Park Service, living history also became a major draw to Shiloh. Over time, a black powder program grew at the battlefield, with volunteers and rangers firing muskets and cannons. The home front was also interpreted, as shown here. A costumed interpreter is cooking at the William Manse George cabin.

In the early years of the park, the best way to reach Shiloh was by riverboat. But with the boom in industrialization and the advent of the automobile, visitors increasingly flocked to the park by car. By the second half of the 20th century, steamboat lines were no longer running, but nostalgic excursions sometimes made stops at Pittsburg Landing. The famous *Delta Queen* occasionally tied up at the landing.

At times, the park's visitation was hampered by natural events such as flooding. Pictured are the original guns denoting the gunboats' action flooded by the Tennessee River. Years of flooding caused so much damage to the causeway that it eventually had to be shut down, and it only reopened to visitors in 2008.

Although the heyday of monumentation was in the first decade of the 1900s, some states continued to erect memorials to their troops under the National Park Service. The State of Texas erected this pink granite monument, similar to those found on other battlefields of the Civil War, during the celebration of the war's centennial in the 1960s. (Courtesy of Brian K. McCutchen.)

Seven

From Centennial to Modernity

Preserving Shiloh

The centennial of the Civil War in the 1960s caused interest in Shiloh and the war to grow over the ensuing decades, with additional commemoration occurring when the states of Kentucky and Missouri placed monuments on the battlefield of Shiloh. Amazingly, it was not until 2005 that the State of Tennessee, the very state in which the battle occurred, dedicated a monument. Fittingly, it is similar in design and overt symbolism to that of memorials erected a century before.

Other forms of memorialization have also continued. Since the 1860s, commemorative services have been held at the national cemetery at Pittsburg Landing, encouraging memory and reunification. Annual Memorial Day services of today hold true to that same premise, honoring soldiers of both North and South, as well as those of all other wars.

Compared to many other American battlefields that have suffered from urban expansion or industry, Shiloh is quite a refreshing locale. The battlefield is similar in appearance to that of the battle period, its remoteness a blessing to its preservation. Historic roads are mostly within their historic matrix, many field lines of the period are as close as can be determined, and key historic features are maintained. More than a century and a half after its entry into popular history, the area around Shiloh Church remains a true American treasure to be preserved for the appreciation and understanding of future generations.

The fabled "Johnston Tree" stood as an article of reverence for many generations. Rot and insects ate away the trunk, and the remains were removed early in the decade of the 2000s. The pieces were placed in the park curatorial collection.

Dedicated in April 1974, the original monument provided by the Commonwealth of Kentucky to honor its troops consisted of two brick pilasters with an aluminum interpretive panel stretching between them. Due to structural issues, granite obelisks replaced the damaged brick in 1989. (Courtesy of Brian K. McCutchen.)

Started as a project by St. Louis–area Boy Scouts, the planning and funding for the Missouri State Monument was a grassroots effort. The monument of red, gray, and blue granite commemorates Missouri's Shiloh soldiers of both sides. It sits adjacent to Wicker Field, where soldiers of the Confederate 1st Missouri Infantry fought against a battery of the Union 1st Missouri Artillery. (Courtesy of Brian K. McCutchen.)

Of the hundreds of thousands of visitors to Shiloh annually, many come as part of special bus tours. Former chief historian of the National Park Service and the author of several Shiloh studies, Edwin C. Bearss, center, has brought the battle to life for countless visitors, perpetuating a fascination for the war that has embraced the nation since the 1860s.

George A. Reaves served as chief of interpretation and resources management at Shiloh from 1975 until his death in 1994. He was instrumental in reanalyzing the Shiloh battle story and its resources, thus encouraging professional historical analysis from all angles rather than simply perpetuating traditional park stories. Park historian Stacy Allen carried forward Reaves's mission to accurately bring Shiloh's history to future generations.

Late-19th-century Memorial Day services and reunion events led to the preservation of the battlefield of Shiloh. Such services continue today, honoring soldiers of both the North and South, as well as veterans of all American wars. In this photograph, Supt. Woody Harrell introduces Congresswoman Marsha Blackburn during the 2006 Memorial Day ceremony.

Shiloh National Military Park has recently seen a major expansion when Congress added a new unit of the park at nearby Corinth, Mississippi, in 2000. The goal was to commemorate the Siege of Corinth and the later battle fought there, as well as the Union occupation, including the site of a contraband camp. The Corinth unit's most obvious improvement is the new interpretive center, seen here.

In June 2005, dedication of the Tennessee State Monument brought to a close more than 15 years of effort to properly honor the soldiers of the Volunteer State at Shiloh. Designed by artist G.L. Sanders, the monument Passing of Honor evokes emotion and symbolism not demonstrated since the veterans themselves erected their monuments more than 80 years earlier. (Courtesy of Brian K. McCutchen.)

The veterans of Shiloh intended that their actions, sacrifices, and lessons be remembered in perpetuity. The stories, books, monuments, and battlefield they set aside are only tools in passing on to future generations an understanding of the importance of their contributions and the seriousness of war, sacrifice, reunification, and freedom. The voices of 1862 are long gone, and thus, it is vital that parents and grandparents of today carry the torch to future generations, such as the three shown here, encouraging them to explore their nation's history, experience their historic sites, and learn of their heritage and the importance and blessings of being an American. (Courtesy of Brian K. McCutchen.)

Bibliography

Allen, Stacy D. "Shiloh!: A Visitor's Guide." *Blue and Gray Magazine* (2001): entire issue.

Cunningham, O. Edward. *Shiloh and the Western Campaign of 1862*. Edited by Gary D. Joiner and Timothy B. Smith. New York: Savas Beatie, 2007.

Daniel, Larry J. *Shiloh: The Battle That Changed the Civil War*. New York: Simon and Schuster, 1997.

Frank, Joseph Allan, and George A. Reaves. *Seeing the Elephant: Raw Recruits at the Battle of Shiloh*. New York: Greenwood Press, 1989; reprinted, Urbana: University of Illinois Press, 2003.

Gentch, James F. "A Geographic Analysis of the Battle of Shiloh." (Master's thesis) Memphis: University of Memphis, 1994.

Isbell, Timothy T. *Shiloh and Corinth: Sentinels of Stone*. Jackson: University Press of Mississippi, 2007.

McCutchen, Brian Keith. "Of Monuments and Remembrance: A History and Structural Analysis of the Monuments of Shiloh." (Master's thesis) Cape Girardeau: Southeast Missouri State University, 1995.

McDonough, James Lee. *Shiloh: In Hell Before Night*. Knoxville: University of Tennessee Press, 1977.

Reed, David W. *The Battle of Shiloh and the Organizations Engaged*. Washington, DC: Government Printing Office, 1902; reprinted with a new introduction by Timothy B. Smith, Knoxville: University of Tennessee Press, 2008.

Smith, Timothy B. *This Great Battlefield of Shiloh: History, Memory, and the Establishment of a Civil War National Military Park*. Knoxville: University of Tennessee Press, 2004.

———. *The Untold Story of Shiloh: The Battle and Battlefield*. Knoxville: University of Tennessee Press, 2006.

Sword, Wiley. *Shiloh: Bloody April*. Revised Edition. Dayton, OH: Morningside Bookshop, 2001.

War of the Rebellion: A Compilation of the Official Records of the Union and Confederate Armies. 128 vols. Washington, DC: Government Printing Office, 1880–1891. Volume 10 contains Shiloh's reports.

Welch, Paul D. *Archeology at Shiloh Indian Mounds, 1899–1999*. Tuscaloosa: University of Alabama Press, 2006.

Woodworth, Steven E., ed. *The Shiloh Campaign*. Carbondale: Southern Illinois University Press, 2009.